Jamestown
SETTLEMENT

RE-CREATING AMERICA'S FIRST PERMANENT ENGLISH SETTLEMENT

On May 14, 1607, thirteen years before the Pilgrims landed in New England, 104 weary men and boys dropped anchor at Jamestown Island to establish a new settlement. They had been traveling from England for almost five months, and were glad to have finally arrived. Sponsored by the Virginia Company of London, the settlers hoped to earn a profit for the Company's stockholders.

The story of the people who founded Jamestown and of the Powhatan Indians they encountered is told at Jamestown Settlement, a unique museum of 17th-century American history and culture. Jamestown Settlement, with its exhibit galleries and re-created outdoor living history areas, is located one mile from the original site of colonization which is preserved and interpreted by the National Park Service and the Association for the Preservation of Virginia Antiquities.

Originally called Jamestown Festival Park, the museum was opened in 1957 to commemorate the 350th anniversary of the establishment of the first permanent English settlement in the New World. In the 1980s plans were made to expand the museum to include exhibits dealing with the culture and contributions of Virginia's Indians. In 1990, Jamestown Settlement reopened with new exhibits, fresh historical interpretations, and exciting artifacts for the public to view.

THE JAMESTOWN SETTLEMENT
Exhibit Galleries

The Jamestown Settlement museum galleries were designed to teach visitors about the background of English settlement, the plans for sailing to Virginia, the American Indians encountered by the English, and the development of the Virginia colony to 1699. Changing exhibits in the temporary gallery explore various themes related to the Jamestown story.

THE ENGLISH GALLERY

In the early 16th century, European trade with other parts of the world flourished. Spain and Portugal were the principal dealers in the trade with the Far East. Spices, silk fabrics, rich woven carpets, dyes, perfumes, and precious stones were much in demand by those who could afford such luxuries. Spain and Portugal also claimed the wealth from lands in the Americas.

English men and women desired such wealth, for individuals as well as for the nation. By the end of the 16th century, private trading companies had received approval from Queen Elizabeth to trade in the Mediterranean, Russia, and the Far East. England began to emerge from her Middle Ages isolation, hoping to challenge Spain's control of the seas.

Sir Walter Raleigh, friend of Queen Elizabeth and promoter of English overseas colonies, was the primary financial backer of the 1580s colony planted at Roanoke. By 1590 the colony had disappeared.

Wahunsonacock, the supreme chief of the Powhatan Indians in Virginia, was described as "a tall well proportioned man, with a sower looke. . . his age neare 60." He ruled over more than 30 Algonquian-speaking tribes in Tidewater Virginia at the time of English settlement.

George Percy was one of the gentlemen in the group of first settlers. Percy recorded descriptions of the voyage of 1607 as well as the starving winter of 1609-10.

Bases in North America would give English privateers a better opportunity to strike at Spanish treasure ships laden with New World gold and silver. Although France had established fur-trading bases in upper North America and Spain held Florida, no country had laid claim to the central coastline of the continent.

Life in England in the late 16th century was difficult for the majority of individuals. A rigid class structure created limited opportunities for economic and social advancement. Wealth and status were tied to the ownership of land. The growing wool trade encouraged landowners to enclose farmlands in order to raise sheep. Small tenant farmers were forced into overcrowded towns and cities. Left with few resources, the lure of wealth, adventure, and a chance for land led these impoverished people to consider taking the risk and going to the New World.

Elizabeth I, the "Virgin Queen," ruled from 1558 to 1603. During her reign, England joined the race for trade and territory.

Technological advances in navigation and ship construction made transoceanic travel to the New World possible.

In the early 17th century, a group of English merchants began to promote plans to colonize Virginia. They sought sources for goods needed in England, markets for English products, and opportunities for new investments. They hoped to find riches and seek a northwest passage to the Orient. In 1606 King James I granted a charter to the Virginia Company, giving the Company a monopoly on trade and investment in North America. In this joint stock company, profits and losses were shared by those who invested by purchasing stock.

The growing wool trade brought large profits to the English economy and to individual merchants, but caused increased poverty among the lower classes.

Shipboard life was difficult, boring, and sometimes dangerous. Passengers coped with an unbalanced diet and cold, unsanitary conditions.

Drawing upon the experiences of prior attempts at colonization, organizers had a vague idea of what was needed for establishing a colony. English colonies had already been attempted in Ireland and at Roanoke in present-day North Carolina in the 1570s and 1580s. The latter, in a new land called Virginia, failed when England's war with Spain prevented the shipping of necessary supplies, and the colonists disappeared. The Virginia Company also benefitted from 16th-century advances in cartography, ship construction, and sailing technology.

By December 1606, three ships and the supplies to support a transatlantic voyage had been procured by the Virginia Company in the city of London. The Company also recruited 105 men and boys to make the initial voyage to Virginia. The ships left London, the gateway to the New World, on a voyage that would take them four and a half months.

By the late 16th century, the European rivals - Spain, Portugal, France, and England - claimed most of the uncharted world. This is a 1606 edition of a 1570 original map by Abraham Ortelius.

THE POWHATAN GALLERY

U pon arrival in Virginia in April 1607, the English encountered the indigenous people of Tidewater Virginia, the Powhatan Indians, with a population of about 14,000. The settlers entered a world that had been populated by humans for thousands of years, a place the people called "Tsenacommacah," the "densely inhabited land." Much of what we know about the Powhatans was recorded by English writers, or has been excavated by archaeologists.

The first Indians inhabited eastern Virginia by 10,000 B.C. These Paleo people lived as wanderers, hunting mastodons and caribou. During the Archaic period, a warmer climate encouraged an increased abundance and variety of food resources, including deer. A more complex culture developed in the Woodland period, with the introduction of crop cultivation and year-round village life.

By the time of European contact, the Powhatan Indians were living in small hamlets and villages. They obtained their food and supplies from the environment, using what was available throughout the year. Agricultural products contributed about half of their diet. The Indians stored little for the winter and spring, living "of what the Country naturally affordeth from hand to mouth." Powhatan men hunted deer and fished, while women farmed and gathered wild plant foods. Women prepared foods and made clothes from deer skins, while both men and women helped in house construction. The environment also provided all the necessary supplies to make tools and equipment—stone, bone, and wood.

The Powhatan Indians of "Tsenacommacah" looked upon the English newcomers with wonder, fear, and interest. They could not foresee how the arrival of these strange people would affect their way of life.

Individually and in large hunting groups, Powhatan men sought the whitetail deer to provide their people with meat, clothing, and tools.

6

The Powhatan chiefdom was comprised of 30-some tribal groups under the control of Wahunsonacock, the "chief ruler," sometimes called "Powhatan." Powhatan's chiefdom or "empire" extended from the Chesapeake Bay to the falls of the James, York, and Rappahannock rivers, and from the south side of the James north to the Rappahannock River. All tribes spoke forms of the Algonquian family of languages.

By about 1580, Wahunsonacock had inherited six tribes through his mother. Over the next 25 years, he conquered 20 or more groups. All tribes paid a yearly tribute to Wahunsonacock to ensure his protection against Indian enemies to the north, west, and south. Most supported him in time of war. Powhatan ruled by a system of customary law, as well as his own commands. Punishments could be severe for those who disobeyed—clubbing or burning to death for major offenses such as theft or murder, and beating for minor offenses.

Villages within the same area belonged to one tribe. Each tribe had its own "werowance" or chief, who was subject to Wahunsonacock. Although chiefs were usually men, they inherited their positions of power through the female side of the family. Chiefs were advised by trusted counselors and priests.

The Powhatans lived in a ranked society of rulers, great warriors, priests, and commoners. Status was determined by achievement, often in warfare, and by the inheritance of high-status goods—copper, shell beads, and furs. Those of higher status had larger homes, more wives, and elaborate dress.

The Powhatan Indians went to war to defend their territory, for revenge, or to capture women and children for adoption into the tribe. Warfare provided men with the opportunity to gain honor and prestige. Most battles were small surprise attacks fought from behind trees or tall grass.

The Powhatans obtained what they needed to live from the environment. They divided the year into five seasons, with a special time for the corn harvest.

Men may have cut and bent the saplings for longhouses, while women wove the mats which covered the "yehakins." Longhouse patterns are found archaeologically throughout eastern Virginia.

Powhatan children learned roles and responsibilities from their elders. Some older boys were chosen for the "huskanaw" ritual, a nine-month ordeal of physical hardship, isolation, and fasting to prepare them for leadership positions. Powhatans married between the ages of 13 and 15. A man paid a bride price to the family of his wife to compensate them for her loss. Wealthy men had more than one wife, and divorce was possible.

The Powhatans enjoyed recreation. Foot races, football games similar to soccer, and gambling games using reeds were popular. They had songs and dances for a variety of occasions—grief, war, and feasting. And they enjoyed making music with reeds, drums, and dried gourds.

Religion played an important role in Powhatan life, but the English had difficulty describing it. The Indians worshipped a hierarchy of gods and spirits. They offered gifts to Oke to prevent him from sending them harm. Ahone was the creator and giver of good things. The bodies of chiefs and priests were preserved and placed on scaffolds in temples, located in larger villages, and maintained by high status priests. Conjurers foretold enemy plans, and cured illnesses with herbs, chants, and treatment in the sweatlodge.

The Powhatans participated in an extensive trade network with Indian groups both within and outside of the chiefdom. Trade was controlled by the elite who used it to increase their social status. Luxury items were traded—copper, shell beads, and pearls. After the arrival of the English, the Powhatans traded foodstuffs and furs in exchange for metal tools, weapons, and European glass beads and copper.

The Powhatans had contact with Europeans prior to the 1607 settlement. In 1570 Spanish Jesuits established a mission on the York River but were killed by local Indians. In the 1580s, English explorers from the Roanoke colony traveled to the mouth of the Bay. Powhatan priests foretold of a prophecy of destruction by invaders. Perhaps they feared this prophecy would come true when Englishmen settled on the James River in 1607.

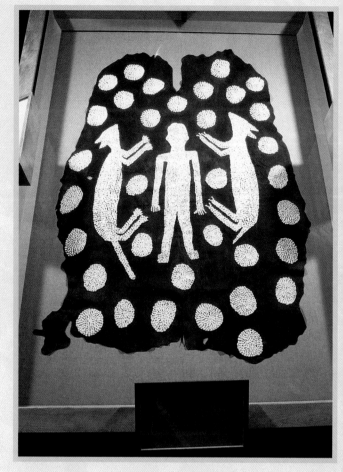

Reproduction of Powhatan's Mantle—The original Powhatan's Mantle, now in the collection of the Ashmolean Museum, Oxford, England, was probably brought to England by John Tradescant, a botanist who visited Virginia in 1637-38. This "robe of the King of Virginia," probably a ceremonial garment, was made from four deer hides and decorated with shell-bead figures. It may have belonged to Wahunsonacock, Powhatan, the supreme chief.

Fish provided the Powhatans with a supplemental food supply when agricultural products and deer meat were low. Men used spears, nets, and traps to catch freshwater and saltwater varieties.

THE JAMESTOWN GALLERY

The first settlers arrived off the coast of Virginia on April 26, 1607. They had been at sea for four months, covering over 6000 miles. The three ships, *Susan Constant*, *Godspeed*, and *Discovery*, took a southwesterly course to the New World. This preferred route used favorable trade winds and ocean currents to carry the settlers from the English Channel, south to the Canary Islands, west to the Caribbean - where the only passenger to die on this trip was lost - and then north to Virginia.

Soon after arrival at Cape Henry, named in honor of King James's son, the colonists erected a cross. Captain Christopher Newport, commander of the expedition, opened a box containing detailed directives from Virginia Company officials to seek a suitable "seating place" for the settlement, as well as a list of the seven individuals who would form the governing council in Virginia—Bartholomew Gosnold, Christopher Newport, John Martin, John Ratcliffe, John Smith, George Kendall, and Edward Maria Wingfield, chosen by the others to serve as president.

The settlers spent two weeks exploring the river they named after King James, and chose a peninsula up river with a deep water anchorage for the ships. On May 14, 1607, they went ashore and began to build Jamestown. The site was selected for its military advantages,

After their arrival, the colonists planted a cross at Cape Henry to verify the English claim to the land, a claim first made at the settlement at Roanoke in the 1580s.

since Jamestown was to be, among other things, a military outpost to check Spanish encroachment in North America. After a skirmish with local Powhatan Indians, the settlers built a triangular palisade with bulwarks at the three corners to hold cannons.

To provide for the 104 settlers who came to Virginia, the colonists began to construct houses within their fort, as well as a church, a storehouse for supplies, and a guardhouse for the soldiers. Early Virginians lived in houses made of riven wood strips covered with clay. Later Virginia houses were covered with clapboards. The large brick mansions of plantations were not built until the second half of the 17th century.

The first settlers living in a new environment soon faced problems of disease. By fall 1607, many of them had died of typhoid fever and dysentery. Many others were weakened by drinking salty water from shallow wells. Only about one-third survived the first winter. Jamestown also struggled with a lack of laborers and supplies from England.

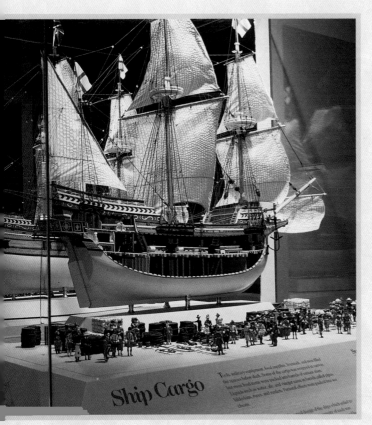

Ship Cargo

The three ships making the original voyage in 1607 were loaded with settlers and supplies for the Virginia Company's venture.

During the first year of the colony, leadership was weak, but was strengthened when Captain John Smith became president in the fall of 1608. Because of his willful personality, however, he was not well-liked. In the fall of 1609, badly injured in a gunpowder explosion, he returned to England and never saw Virginia again.

Smith's contributions to the success of the early colony are numerous. His records of the early colony and the Powhatan Indians are superior to any others of the period. His map of the Chesapeake region, including the sites of Powhatan villages, stood alone until the mid-17th century. His diplomacy with Powhatan gained the colony much-needed foodstuffs during several hungry periods.

John Smith first met Pocahontas, Powhatan's daughter, in December 1607, when he was captured and brought to her father's village, Werowocomoco. Smith later wrote that he believed Powhatan intended to kill him, but Pocahontas intervened and saved his life. Smith probably was put through a ritual, in which Powhatan hoped to intimidate, but not kill the Englishman. He was adopted as Powhatan's "son," and favorable diplomatic relations continued for a time.

Pocahontas was Powhatan's favorite daughter. As Smith's special guardian, she felt a great loss at his return to England. In 1613 she was kidnapped by the English who hoped to exchange her for English prisoners held by Powhatan. When her father refused, she remained with the English, studied Anglican religion, and was baptized with the name "Rebecca." She married John Rolfe in 1614, and had a son, Thomas, in 1615. A year later, to encourage financial support for the Virginia venture, Company officials sent Pocahontas and her family to London. There, she became sick. Just as the group was ready to return to Virginia in 1617, Pocahontas died and was buried at Gravesend, England.

When John Smith was in Virginia, relations with the Powhatan Indians were tenuous, but trade flourished. While the English needed food and wanted furs for the English market, the Powhatans wanted metal tools, weapons, copper pots, and European glass beads. When Smith left, however, the Indians lost a reliable trader. The arrival of 400 more settlers in late summer resulted in the first Anglo-Powhatan war. Over the winter of 1609-10, the Indians' "starving siege" made it impossible for the English to leave James Fort for food, reducing the English population from about 300 to 90 by spring. In 1614, peaceful relations were established which lasted until 1622.

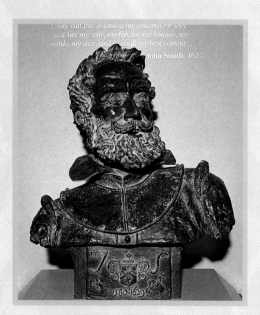

Although he only lived in Virginia two years, Captain John Smith was an able leader, cartographer, historian, and promoter of the colony until his death in 1631. The bust was sculpted by Robert S.S. Baden-Powell in 1900 and is owned by The Library of Virginia.

The military presence was necessary at Jamestown as a deterrent against Spanish attack from the south, or threats from local Indians.

Pocahontas lived between two worlds after her capture by the English. She married the Englishman John Rolfe and helped bring attention to the struggling colony.

Ætatis suæ 21. A. 1616.

Rebecka daughter to the mighty Prince iperour of Attanoughkomouck als Virginia nd baptized in the Chriftian faith, and the wor." M" Tho: Rolff.

Trade established with the Powhatan Indians kept the colony alive. They provided corn, deer, and other foodstuffs in exchange for metal tools, weapons, beads, and trinkets.

In 1616 the Virginia Company began distributing large tracts of land to its stockholders, who sought payment on their investments, and by 1622, these "particular plantations" lined the James River. Further, under the "head-right" system, a person who paid for another's transportation to Virginia was entitled to fifty acres of land.

These land grants pushed the Powhatans to revolt. Following Powhatan's death, his brother and successor, Opechancanough, organized a revolt which, in one day in 1622, killed more than one-fourth of the English settlers at plantations along the James River. A resulting series of retaliatory events continued over ten years. A third Powhatan uprising in 1644 made little impact upon the enlarged English settlement. Within a short period, the Powhatan Indians were reduced to reservations, and their numbers dwindled throughout the remainder of the 17th century.

The English in Virginia hoped to obtain raw materials needed for English industries. In the beginning, Polish and German workers attempted the production of pitch and pine tar, sassafras for medicine, glass, and wood products for the shipbuilding and housing industries in England. The Company sent Italians and Frenchmen to establish wine and silk making. However, none of these early attempts brought profits.

In 1610, John Rolfe appeared in Virginia. Famous for his 1614 marriage to Pocahontas, Rolfe is the man who introduced tobacco cultivation to the colony. The Powhatans grew a bitter native tobacco, but Englishmen had become accustomed to a good, sweet smoke from Spanish tobacco. Rolfe experimented with some seed and, within a few years, produced a crop that brought high prices in England. Everyone in Virginia wanted to plant the "weed."

By the 1620s the "golden weed" had become Virginia's cash crop. Tobacco was used to pay for everything—necessities as well as luxury goods, debts, and services rendered. But the prices fetched by tobacco did not always reflect the great deal of land and labor that it required. Because it quickly depleted the soil of nutrients, large tracts of land were necessary. And it was a year-round proposition, requiring a large labor supply.

Initially, tobacco planters acquired indentured servants to work in their tobacco fields. After fulfilling an indenture of four to seven years, these people were free, but landless, and many became tenant farmers until they were able to acquire their own property. By mid-17th century, conditions in England improved, and fewer English people wanted to indenture themselves in Virginia. Tobacco planters were forced to find another form of labor, and turned to African slaves from the West Indies.

The first Africans came to Virginia in 1619. Initially they became indentured servants much like their English counterparts. Some completed their indentures and acquired their own land and servants. However, by mid-century, tobacco planters began acquiring African servants and holding them for life, creating a system of slavery in the colony. In the early 1660s the first Virginia laws regulating slavery were written. The legalization of slavery brought increasingly limited opportunities for African Americans.

The average Virginian was of the "middling sort"—small tobacco planters, tenant farmers, and craftsmen. Households consisting of several children and several indentured servants changed constantly due to births, deaths, and remarriages, which brought with them step-parents and step-siblings. By the late 1600s social mobility had decreased, and power was concentrated in the hands of a few wealthy men, primarily tobacco planters/merchants, who often served on the governor's council of advisers.

The numbers of women in the colony were scarce throughout the century, with the men outnumbering the women three to one. Some women followed their husbands to the New World, or came as indentured servants. In 1620 a large number were sent by the Virginia Company to become wives for planters. Married women had limited legal rights. Their primary responsibilities were in child care and in running the household.

In the early years of the colony, the Virginia Company

The first laborers were indentured servants, but tobacco planters came to rely upon African slaves from the West Indies by the mid-17th century.

governed Virginia. In 1619 Virginians were granted the right to elect officials to a House of Burgesses, the colony's first law-making body. Financial troubles and the 1622 Indian uprising led King James I to abolish the Virginia Company in 1624, and to declare Virginia a royal colony, led by a governor appointed by the king.

The Church of England was the state church, with little room for religious dissidents. Conformity to Anglican rituals and financial support of the Church were required by law. In 1693 King William and Queen Mary granted a charter to establish the College of William and Mary for the education of Virginia youth.

Jamestown remained the capital of the Virginia colony until 1699 when a fire destroyed the statehouse. The seat of government was moved to Middle Plantation which was renamed Williamsburg. Jamestown reverted to farmland. The island was used during the Civil War by Confederate forces. In 1893 the owners gave 22 acres to the Association for the Preservation of Virginia Antiquities, and the remainder became the property of the National Park Service in 1934. The role of Jamestown in the founding of Virginia has been celebrated over the years through archaeological investigations, pilgrimages, and festivals.

Because men outnumbered women in Virginia three to one, women were highly valued. A married woman had few legal rights, and a household full of chores.

Sweet-scented tobacco, the "golden weed," became Virginia's cash crop. Colonists sought land and labor to become planters.

THE INDIAN VILLAGE

The Powhatan Indian Village at Jamestown Settlement is representative of a small hamlet, typical of the way that most of the Powhatans were living at the time of the English colonization of Virginia. Larger villages where werowances or chiefs lived had specialized structures such as a large chief's house, a temple, storage buildings, and perhaps a palisade. A hamlet, with less than ten houses, was not the residence of a tribal chief. Hamlets had ordinary dwellings and smaller storage structures.

The Powhatan Indians who lived in a hamlet resided in longhouses called "yehakins" which measured about 12 by 16 feet. These houses were built by bending young saplings, and covering them with bark or mats woven from reeds. Low wooden frames for sleeping lined the inside walls of the houses. An indoor fire was used for warmth and for cooking in inclement weather. Some houses had storage racks to hold equipment and foodstuffs.

Activities in a hamlet centered upon maintaining daily life. During the spring and summer months, much time was spent by women and children in the fields, planting and weeding crops of corn, beans, squash, and sunflowers. In the early fall, they harvested these crops, drying many of them for later use. The women made breads and hominy out of the corn and used the other crops with meat in stews. Some of the crops were given as a tribute to the chief who lived in a larger adjacent village. He in turn owed an annual tribute to Wahunsonacock, or Powhatan, the supreme chief of the Powhatan Indians.

The English described Powhatan houses as dry, warm, and smoky. Frames or racks built along the inside served as beds.

Smaller Powhatan villages or hamlets consisted of less than ten longhouses called yehakins, each built to house one nuclear family.

The fall harvest was a time of celebration. The Powhatans had a separate, or fifth season of the year just for the corn harvest. Feasting, dancing, and singing occurred in hamlets and villages, perhaps around a dancing face circle.

When men were not hunting or fishing, they spent time in the hamlet making and repairing tools and weapons for the fall and winter hunting seasons. They primarily used bow and arrow for hunting deer, turkey, and small game. In the winter, men joined in large communal hunts for deer near the fall line. Most of the camp moved to the hunting grounds in order to be able to process the deer immediately.

Men also made stone and bone points for longer spears which they used in spring fishing. Nets made of natural cordage and weirs or traps of saplings were also used to catch both fresh and saltwater fish. Men also worked on canoes, the Powhatans' main form of transportation. Most canoes were made of cypress and were up to 50 feet long.

Throughout the leaner months of late winter and early spring, the Powhatans relied heavily upon gathered wild foods. Most Powhatan

Women and children cared for the crops of corn, beans, and squash using tools made from wood and bone. Children may have sat in the scarecrow hut to drive away predators. Agricultural produce contributed about half of the Powhatan diet.

adults had a wide knowledge of the variety of edible wild plants, roots, nuts, berries, and grains. Along with fishing, they depended upon what they could gather until summer when they could rely upon their agricultural crops.

Most cooking was done over fires outside, except in inclement weather. Powhatans stored most of their possessions inside their houses.

Harvested crops included corn, beans, squash, and sunflower seeds. Powhatan women dried many of the crops for later use.

Powhatan men fished with spears, traps, and nets made of cordage. They sought both fresh and saltwater varieties.

Deer provided hides for clothing and blankets. The hair was removed with shell or stone scrapers if the garment was for summer use. It was then tanned using deer brains and smoked to make it waterproof and soft.

The Powhatan people took everything they needed from the local environment. Deer not only provided meat, but skins for clothing, bones for tools and weapons, and sinew for fastening tool and weapon parts. Local and traded stone materials were worked into celts and axes for cutting and chopping, mortars and pestles for grinding, and flaked into arrow and spear points for hunting. Local clays were fashioned into pottery vessels used for cooking and storage. The forest supplied an abundance of wood used in house construction, agricultural tools, and weapons.

Powhatan women made clothing out of deer hides which had been scraped and tanned to soften them. The hair was kept on for winter garments. Everyone wore a type of garment like an apron and added more skins and leggings when cold weather came. The Indians also covered their bodies with bear grease for extra warmth.

Powhatan men usually wore nothing more than a loin cloth, and women only wore a lower-body apron, but in cooler weather more garments were added. Clothes often were decorated with shells, beads, and paint.

Adult life started at an early age for Powhatan Indians. Children learned their roles in life by watching their parents. Young children may have guarded the fields, perhaps from the platform of a scarecrow hut. Marriage took place between the ages of 13 and 15.

Each household in a hamlet held a nuclear family of father, mother, and children. John Smith noted that up to 20 people lived together, but he probably observed the families of the elite who could support more than one wife and their children at a time. Status and descent were determined through the female line.

Hamlets and villages in the same area were made up of people from one tribe. Chiefs resided in the villages. The people who lived within a specific tribal district probably came together for ceremonies and traveled for social and economic purposes. Thus hamlet dwellers would have come into contact with larger villages and their related structures. In times of war, the men of a hamlet fought with their tribal chief, who usually allied himself with the other Powhatan tribes under Wahunsonacock.

Tools were made from materials gathered locally, or from stone traded from tribes farther away. Men shaped axes and arrow and spear points by grinding, chipping, and flaking.

Powhatan men spent time in the villages making and repairing their tools and weapons. Some important tools were the bow and arrow, used primarily for hunting game.

Powhatan Indians worshipped a hierarchy of gods and spirits. Perhaps on a daily basis they made offerings, particularly to one of their chief gods, Oke, in order to appease him and obtain his favor. They thanked Ahone, their other named god, for his goodness. Individual hamlets may have had some lower class priests called cockarouses, who foretold the future and helped to cure illnesses.

The Indian Village (hamlet) at Jamestown Settlement does not represent any particular settlement in the Powhatan chiefdom. It is a re-creation, based upon extensive archaeological work done in eastern Virginia in the 1980s and 1990s. Other information comes from descriptions written by early settlers such as John Smith, and watercolors of coastal Algonquians painted by John White, governor of the Roanoke colony in the 1580s.

The Powhatan Indians have left a legacy through their descendants still living in Virginia. Today the Commonwealth of Virginia recognizes seven Powhatan tribes—Chickahominy, Eastern Chickahominy, Mattaponi, Nansemond, Pamunkey, United Rappahannock, and Upper Mattaponi. The Pamunkey and Mattaponi have state reservations. Virginia also recognizes the Monacan tribe, a people of the Virginia Piedmont.

Powhatan men made canoes from cypress logs. They burned out the inside and scraped away the charred remains with shell and stone scrapers.

Women fashioned pots from local clay. The pots had "egg-shaped" bottoms to allow them to be set down in the hot coals of a fire. Decoration resulted from the paddling process, using either corncobs or paddles wrapped with cordage.

The Powhatan Indians of Virginia may have had dancing face circles like the Algonquian Indians of coastal North Carolina, who used them for ceremonies such as harvest festivals.

Powhatan men went to war for revenge, to defend their territory, or to capture women and children for adoption into the tribe. Most battles were surprise attacks fought from behind trees with clubs.

THE SHIPS

The three ships at Jamestown Settlement represent the original vessels which brought the first settlers to Virginia in 1607. On December 20, 1606, three English ships set sail from London. *Susan Constant*, commanded by Captain Christopher Newport, was only one year old. *Godspeed*, commanded by Bartholomew Gosnold, and *Discovery*, commanded by John Ratcliffe were leased or purchased for the voyage. They carried a total of 144 men and boys, 104 of whom would establish the settlement in Virginia.

A popular course to Virginia led ships south to the Canary Islands and across the Atlantic to the Caribbean, where reprovisions could be acquired. Although this route took advantage of trade winds and currents, ships were at sea for two to four months.

The 1607 voyage from England to Virginia was only one of many that involved the transportation of colonists across the Atlantic to the colonies in America. Generally, ships of the early 17th-century were small and cramped by 20th-century standards. They relied on sail power; if the winds did not blow, the ships did not move.

One reason for choosing Jamestown Island was its deep-water anchorage.

Early 17th-century ships with a mixed sail plan of square and lateen or triangular sails resulted in easier maneuverability.

Early 17th-century wooden merchant ships were designed to be longer than previous vessels, making them faster and more maneuverable. Deeper hulls and a mixed sail plan of square and lateen or triangular sails improved speed and turning. The development of the whipstaff, a length of wood fastened to the tiller, which in turn moved the rudder, enabled the steersman to maneuver the tiller. In the 18th century the whipstaff would be replaced by the ship's wheel.

The main deck was the center of activity. The Great Cabin housed the captain, and the steersman worked and slept in the steerage room. The cooking room was in the forecastle. Most of the officers had berths in cabins on the main deck.

The navigator used devices such as the cross-staff to determine the ship's latitudinal position, by measuring the angle of the sun and completing a mathematical computation. Celestial navigation was difficult on the deck of a pitching, rolling ship.

Sailors could employ the capstan, used for raising and lowering the anchor, to lift heavy barrels and other cargo from the hold.

Below the main deck was the 'tween deck, packed with cargo, cannon and accessories, and passengers. In the 'tween deck, passengers and sometimes "common" sailors slept on pallets or mattresses. Wealthier passengers may have obtained a "hanging cabin" made of canvas suspended from hooks, allowing more privacy.

Below this deck was the cargo hold, where supplies, livestock, and goods to be shipped back were stored. At the very bottom of the ship was the ballast, stones or gravel which prevented the ship from capsizing.

The tasks of sailing filled much of the time for the ship's crew. The master or captain supervised the voyage; the pilot directed the course near land; the navigator directed the course at sea; and the carpenter did repairs. Other members of the crew were responsible for the rigging, the cooking, and maintaining the armament.

The men responsible for common duties were the sailors, who worked in four-hour shifts, called watches. Often, their wages were held until the ship reached its final destination. Their living quarters were cramped and unhealthy, and many men developed scurvy and other diseases.

Food could only be cooked at sea if the weather was calm. An unbalanced diet, poor nutrition, and spoiled rations often led to debilitating sicknesses.

Sailors determined the depth of the water with an instrument called the lead line.

SUSAN CONSTANT STATISTICS

Year built	1990
Overall length	116'
Beam of hull	24' 10"
Mainmast Height	95'
Tonnage	120
Passengers in 1607	54 (est.)
Crew in 1607	17 (est.)

GODSPEED STATISTICS

Year built	1984
Overall length	68'
Beam of hull	14' 8"
Mainmast Height	55'
Tonnage	40
Passengers in 1607	39 (est.)
Crew in 1607	13 (est.)

Passengers had to spend most of their time in the 'tween deck, where space was limited, odors lingered, and time passed slowly. They shared this space with cannon, some of the crew, and all of their belongings.

Because they did not help in sailing the ships, passengers had a lot of time to spend gambling with cards, dice, or draughts (checkers), playing musical instruments, or telling stories.

DISCOVERY STATISTICS

Year built	1984
Overall length	49' 6"
Beam of hull	11' 4"
Mainmast Height	42'
Tonnage	20
Passengers in 1607	12 (est.)
Crew in 1607	9 (est.)

The health of sea travelers was precarious, due to overcrowding, disease, and poor nutrition. While the English diet was fairly well balanced, lack of storage space and inadequate preservation limited the types of food carried. Cooking could be done only in fair weather in an iron cooking box which was lined with bricks.

Foods that could be kept for weeks and months were carried at sea, preserved by salting, drying, and pickling in vinegar. Basic daily rations included dried hardtack or ship's biscuit, salted, dried or pickled meats and fish, cheese, oatmeal or barley, and a gallon of beer or cider. Officers and gentlemen may have had more extravagant foods and wine.

If a ship passed by land, it usually stopped for fresh provisions. The 1607 voyage to Virginia stopped in the Caribbean where the ships picked up fish, fowl, sea tortoises, wild boars, fruits and vegetables. On long voyages, much of the food became spoiled—the biscuit moldy, the meat full of maggots, the beer watery, and the water contaminated.

The unwholesome environment created health problems for all. Scurvy brought the most irritation. Caused by a lack of vitamin C, "the plague of the sea" produced bleeding gums and general enfeeblement. Many travelers contracted dysentery from poor drinking water.

Although conditions on the 1607 voyage were less than desirable, passenger George Percy noted that only one person died, Edward Brookes, succumbing to heat stroke in the Caribbean. Other voyages were not so lucky. On the 1609 fleet to Virginia, 32 people died of "calenture," or tropical fevers.

Passengers had no duties on ships and a great deal of free time. They may have filled these empty hours storytelling, gambling at cards or dice, draughts (checkers) or dominoes, or playing musical instruments. To help maintain morale, religious services were a regular part of most ships' routines. Some ships, such as those on the 1607 voyage, carried chaplains.

The main deck of a sailing ship was filled with a variety of activities, setting the sails and rigging, lifting and lading cargo, and doing general repairs.

Sailors established the ship's position at sea by determining their speed—using sand glass and logline, their direction—using the compass, and their latitude—using the crosstaff or astrolabe.

Seamen had to work as a team to set more than 100 lines of rigging on an early 17th-century vessel.

The captain and officers had specific quarters for sleeping and storing their personal items.

Traveling to the New World was costly for passengers. The chances of shipwreck, sickness, or death were great. The monetary cost was high as well. An individual paid to transport himself across the Atlantic. If he could not pay, the Virginia Company or another person paid the charges, and the passenger had to serve a period of indenture after reaching the colony.

Once the Jamestown colony was established in June 1607, Captain Newport and his crew sailed for England, leaving only *Discovery* behind. Merchant ships were a lifeline to home for the settlers in Virginia, bringing fresh supplies, more colonists, and news from England.

Little is known about the ships which sailed to Virginia in 1607. Records indicate that *Susan Constant* was built in 1605. The tonnage or carrying capacity of each ship was recorded, and was used by maritime historians along with contemporary paintings and documentary material to determine the dimensions and basic shape of the replicas at Jamestown Settlement.

The Jamestown Settlement ships are sailed in an active sailing program which involves many volunteer sailors. In 1985, Godspeed reenacted the 1607 voyage from England to Virginia.

JAMES FORT

T The triangular James Fort standing today is a re-creation of the 1610 fort described by an early English colonist. The first fort at Jamestown was built soon after the English landed at Jamestown Island in May 1607. This first fort was triangular with the main gate facing the river, and had bulwarks or raised areas at each corner to support cannon.

Once the palisade walls were in place, the colonists began construction of the buildings inside the fort. Their instructions required them to build the "public buildings" first—the storehouse, church, and guardhouse. A church was essential to the expression of their Anglican faith. The storehouse was necessary to house imported supplies, as well as to store exports to be shipped to England. The guardhouse was used as a headquarters for those on guard duty.

During the first months, some colonists lived in tents, some in makeshift houses. The first houses constructed by the colonists were built in a style familiar in England—wattle and daub. After framing a house, horizontal pieces of riven wood were woven between the vertical frames. Clay mixed with water, sand, and straw was applied to the wattle. The houses were thatched with bundles of local marsh reeds, or covered with riven clapboard. Each house probably served six to eight people, primarily men.

After a fire burned the first fort in January 1608, Captain John Smith wrote that rebuilding it reduced it to a "five square plan," perhaps a pentagonal shape. In 1610 when Lord De La Warr arrived in the colony, he ordered repairs to the fort, again making it triangular, built of "planckes and strong posts." William Strachey, a colonist, described three streets along the palisades, with a marketplace, and three public buildings.

Sawyers prepared lumber for building Jamestown and for shipping back to England, where wood products were in short supply.

James Fort was a triangular palisade with three bulwarks for placing artillery. In the first years of settlement, the houses and public buildings were contained within the palisade.

One of the three public buildings, the guardhouse served as headquarters for those assigned to guard duty. Swords, matchlock muskets, and body armor were necessary for defense in Virginia.

Activities in and about James Fort from 1607 to 1614 centered upon survival, military drills, and the demands placed by constant influxes of settlers. Also, settlers hoped to find ways to make economic profits for the Virginia Company, the colony's financial backer. The colonists also attempted to transfer their social customs and beliefs to their new colony.

Life was difficult for the colonists in the early years at Jamestown. About one-third of the first group died in the fall of 1607 from dysentery and typhoid fever. Supply ships came sporadically, and not always when they were needed. The colony depended heavily upon tools and equipment from England.

Because many of the first group of settlers were gentlemen who had organizational and military skills, but did not do manual work, many jobs were left undone. Other groups of early colonists had skills that proved useless— gold refiners, perfumers, and jewelers. Within a few years John Smith realized that the Company needed to send more carpenters, masons, blacksmiths, farmers, and general laborers.

The colonists did not immediately begin growing food for themselves because of a lack of farmers, but relied on trade with the Powhatan Indians for corn and meat. This kept them fed until the winter of 1609-10, when the Powhatans laid seige to James Fort, preventing settlers from going outside to obtain food. Many starved that winter.

The few women in Jamestown cooked, sewed, and maintained livestock and "kitchen" gardens, in which they grew vegetables and herbs.

27

English women cooked over an open hearth, preparing traditional English meals but adapting recipes to foods available in Virginia.

The typical Jamestown house was made of wattle and daub, covered with a roof of thatch, or marsh reeds.

When martial law was imposed upon the colony by the Company in 1610, the colonists were forced to work hard and feed themselves to ensure their survival. The most common work to be done was farming, and with the opening up of new settlements up and down James River, the settlers took over lands that had been cleared by the Powhatans for planting food crops.

Carpenters worked at building houses and cutting wood products for shipment back to England. Polish and German workers tried extractive industries such as glassmaking, pitch and tar production, and potash for soap-making. And imported Frenchmen tried silk and wine making. Perhaps a few others worked at blacksmithing, primarily repairing tools and weapons for the use of the tradesmen and the soldiers.

Military drills took up much of the men's time. At first, only a portion were professional soldiers, supported by the gentlemen who had military experience in Europe and Ireland in the late 16th century. After 1609, however, every man was required to train daily in the use of the musket, sword, and the wearing of armor. A colonial militia comprised of all free white males was not organized until 1622.

Women were in short supply in the first few years. Two, Mistress Forest and Ann Burras, her maid, came in October 1608. Ann Burras married John Laydon shortly after her arrival, and the Laydon family survived into the 1630s in Virginia. Other women came in the 1609-10 supply, and a large group was sent in 1620 to become wives for planters.

Although there were few women, those who were here probably performed duties familiar to them in England, centered around the house. They planted "kitchen" gardens, growing vegetables and herbs for cooking and medicinal purposes. They did most of the cooking, sewing, and laundry, and often tended livestock such as chickens, goats, cows, and pigs.

Daily meals offered a break from work. Traditionally, the Englishman's main meal was dinner, served at noon. It was commonly made up of meat such as pork, poultry, or seafood, some type of bread, made from cornmeal in Virginia, and cider, wine, or ale. The other meals of the day consisted of bread and "pottage" or stew made up of vegetables and grains.

The Fort blacksmith repaired tools and military equipment. In the first years, he probably produced very little equipment, since most tools and weapons were brought from England.

Triangular James Fort was constructed immediately after the colonists' arrival in 1607. The fort provided protection from the Indians. Each corner had a raised area, or bulwark, to support a cannon. Before 1610 only a portion of the men were professional soldiers. After that, all men were required to train daily in muskets and sword use and the wearing of armor.

In Virginia's forests, matchlock muskets were the most effective weapon of defense. Swords and pole arms were useful in close-range combat.

John Rolfe began experimenting with tobacco cultivation around 1610, and it very quickly became Virginia's "golden weed."

Another business for many of the men in Jamestown was government. Since the town was the capital of a growing colony, the governor and his advisory council met there periodically. Courts would have met there too. During the period of martial law, however, civil laws and courts were replaced by harsh military requirements and punishments. Military law technically lasted until 1619 when the colonists were granted the right to elect officials, called burgesses, to the first legislative assembly in English America. Virginia became a royal colony in 1624 and then fell under the rule of the king.

Church attendance was important to English life. The early Virginia colonists did not come to the New World for religious freedom as the Pilgrims did thirteen years later. They worshipped in the Church of England, or Anglican Church, and brought its practices with them. All colonists were required to attend church twice a day. There was little or no religious toleration in Virginia in the 17th century.

The settlers brought with them their forms of recreation. They probably played musical instruments such as the recorder. Some gambling likely occurred over card games, dice games such as hazzard, and board games such as backgammon, draughts (checkers), or nine men's morris. When Sir Thomas Dale arrived at Jamestown in 1611, he found men bowling in the streets, probably either a form of lawn bowling, or nine pins.

The settlers' lives were changed by the introduction of tobacco by John Rolfe around 1610. Within a few years, tobacco prices rose in England and colonists wanted to grow their own tobacco. In 1614, three acre tracts of land were granted to settlers, who were required to grow corn along with their tobacco, and to give a certain percentage of the corn back to the government.

By 1617 the Virginia Company began giving out larger tracts to Company shareholders who had been promised a return on their investments. These new landowners sent settlers to plantations along the James River to grow tobacco. More workers were needed for the tobacco fields, so English and African-American indentured servants were procured in the 1620s.

The settlers were members of the Church of England, and were required by law to attend two services a day. The first legislative assembly met in the Jamestown Church in 1619.

The encroachment onto Indian lands caused the Powhatan Indians to grow angry. They revolted in 1622, in the second Anglo-Powhatan War, killing more than one-fourth of the English colonists.

Jamestown began to grow outside the fort walls after 1614, when the first Anglo-Powhatan War ended. Settlement on the island spread east into an area that came to be called New Town. The eastern-most part of the island was farmed by several major landholders. Jamestown remained the capital of the growing agricultural colony until 1699.

The fort at Jamestown Settlement today is built about one mile away from the site of the original 1607 palisade. This re-created fort is based upon descriptions by set-tlers John Smith, George Percy, and William Strachey, as well as a rudimentary outline of James Fort on an English map currently housed in the Spanish archives, Seville, Spain. The fort buildings are based upon archaeological excavations of early 17th century Chesapeake area houses, as well as late 16th and early 17th century houses still in existence in England.

Today the original site of James Fort is administered by the Association for the Preservation of Virginia Antiquities, an organization which shares the preservation of Jamestown Island with the National Park Service. Current excavations by the APVA are attempting to determine the exact location of the original palisade.

Riven clapboard was made to ship to England for house construction. By the 1620s, Virginians were covering their houses with clapboard, because of the abundance of timber.